Pixie & Fenway

Unlikely Friends at Two Mountain Farm

Karen E. Rose

For my brother, Doug.

We were an example of how two
very different people could
still be great friends.

I miss my friend

This is a true story,

Take it from me.

I am the Farm Mom,

And with my eyes I see.

A chicken and cat,

Such a mismatched pair.

But though they are different,

A kind friendship they share.

So find a comfy seat,

And lend a keen ear.

A true story of friendship,

Is what you are about to hear.

Pixie is a Chicken.

Pixie came to live at Two Mountain Farm as a baby chick with 25 of her baby chick friends.

Pixie and all the chicks lived together in the chicken house. They grew soft feathers, learned to cluck, laid eggs and grew up to be hens.

Fenway is a big furry Cat

Fenway lives in the farm house.
His favorite room is the screened porch.
He can watch the birds, squirrels, and
chipmunks. He can even hear the
chickens clucking.

One day after eating lunch, the Farm Mom went down to the chicken house to collect eggs. "Oh my goodness," she cried out.

Pixie was lying on the floor. Her friends had picked on her and pulled out her feathers on her neck and wings.

The Farm Mom scooped Pixie up and quickly brought her into the farm house.

The Farm Mom decided that Pixie needed to live in a smaller chicken coop on the screened porch so that she would not be picked on anymore.

After a few days, Pixie looked stronger and felt better. The Farm Mom let Pixie out of her coop to walk around the screened porch and stretch her legs.

Just as Pixie started exploring, Fenway
came out onto the screened porch as he did
every morning.

Fenway walked right up to Pixie, sniffed her
from her feet up to her beak and said, "Hi,
my name is Fenway and I am a cat."

Pixie replied, "Hi, I am a chicken and my name is Pixie."

"Why are you out on my screened porch?" asked Fenway.

"Our Farm Mom brought me up here to live because my chicken friends picked on me and pulled out my feathers," said Pixie.

"If they are your friends, why would they pick on you?" asked Fenway.

"I don't know. I was always nice to them," Pixie said sadly, "they were supposed to be my friends."

Fenway tilted his head and looked at Pixie, "Well, are we supposed to be friends?"

"I am not sure, you don't look like a chicken," Pixie replied.

"And you don't look like a cat. You have wings and I have paws," said Fenway

"I have a beak, and you have a nose and whiskers," noticed Pixie.

Fenway looked at Pixie, "I meow when I talk and you cluck. You are also covered in feathers and my coat is made of fur."

"We sure have a lot of differences," Pixie said shaking her head, "maybe we should not be friends."

Fenway thought about this for a minute, "Well, I think I would like to be friends with you Pixie. You seem very nice and I don't mind at all if you live on the screened porch; I would be happy to share my room with you."

After just a few days of sharing the screened
porch, Pixie and Fenway discovered lots of
new things about each other.

Pixie asked Fenway, "Why do you sit and
look out the window?"

"I love watching the birds and chipmunks,"
said Fenway.

"Why do you sometimes go into that box in your coop?" Fenway asked Pixie.

"I go in there to lay my egg," replied Pixie

"Wow, that's neat," said Fenway, "we cats don't lay eggs. There sure are lots of things that are different about us Pixie."

As the months passed and the seasons changed, Pixie and Fenway's friendship grew.

In the warmer months, the door from the farm house to the screened porch was left open so Fenway could go in and out whenever he wanted.

Although Pixie was not allowed in the farm house, Fenway would never tell on Pixie when she would sneak in through the open door to visit with Fenway.

Sometimes though, the Farm Mom would know that Pixie had been in the house because Pixie pooped on the floor! Fenway and Pixie would always giggle about that; they were not so sneaky after all.

Fenway always looked out for Pixie. When a mouse would try to eat Pixie's food, Fenway would chase it away.

During the cooler months, Pixie would get warm rice and warm water for breakfast. Fenway just loved drinking from Pixie's water bowl and Pixie would always share her warm water with him.

"It's like a hot cup of tea in the morning," Fenway said, "I really enjoy sharing breakfast with you."

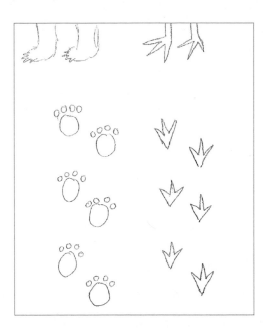

In the winter months when the snow
blew in onto the screened porch, Pixie and
Fenway would play in the snow and make
silly footprints; chicken feet and kitty paws.

Sometimes, Pixie and Fenway would just sit and listen to the falling rain as they dozed off for a nap.

"I wonder what adventures we will have and what new friends we will meet on the farm?" wondered Fenway as his eyes got sleepy.

"I am not sure," answered Pixie, "but it will be fun to experience them with you Fenway. I am so glad that we became friends."

"Me too," replied Fenway, "goodnight my friend."

"Goodnight," Pixie clucked as she snoozed off to sleep dreaming of more fun times and new friends at Two Mountain Farm.

With Much Gratitude To:

🐾 Bryan who introduced me to chicken keeping and indulges my whims when it comes to their comfort and care. I am so thankful to have such a partner; much love.

🐾 Murray McMurray Hatchery for the quality flock of chickens that live at Two Mountain Farm; including Pixie.

🐾 The Connecticut Humane Society for giving people like me a wonderful facility and avenue to adopt pets like Fenway.

🐾 The community of family and friends who supported and encouraged me to tell Pixie and Fenway's story.

🐾 All the kid artists who helped me visually tell a story of an unlikely friendship through a different creative eye.

🖤 My Mom and Dad who created a home environment that fostered appreciation and respect for differences; in people, ideas, philosophy, and much more. I am forever grateful for that life lesson and for your love and support.

Index of Artists

Made in the USA
Middletown, DE
13 May 2016